Also by Maureen Seaton

Sweet World (2019)

Fisher (2018)

Tit, with Blue Guitar (chapbook) (2016)

Fibonacci Batman: New & Selected Poems 1991-2011 (2013)

Genetics (2012)

Cave of the Yellow Volkswagen (2009)

America Loves Carney (chapbook) (2009)

Sex Talks to Girls: A Memoir (2008)

Venus Examines Her Breast (2004)

Little Ice Age (2001)

Miss Molly Rockin' (chapbook) (1998)

Furious Cooking (1996)

The Sea among the Cupboards (1992)

Fear of Subways (1991)

Co-authored

Zero-Zero (chapbook, with Kristine Snodgrass) (2021)

Myth America: Poems in Collaboration (chapbook, with Carolina Hospital, Nicole Hospital-Medina, & Holly Iglesias) (2020)

Road to the Multiverse (chapbook, with Samuel Ace) (2020)

Caprice: Collected, Uncollected, and New Collaborations (with Denise Duhamel) (2015)

Madame Curie's Cookbook (chapbook, with Samuel Ace) (2013)

Two Thieves & a Liar (with Neil de la Flor & Kristine Snodgrass) (2012)

Sinéad O'Connor and Her Coat of a Thousand Bluebirds (with Neil de la Flor) (2011)

Stealth (with Samuel Ace) (2011)

Facial Geometry (chapbook, with Neil de la Flor & Kristine Snodgrass) (2006)

Little Novels (chapbook, with Denise Duhamel) (2002)

Oyl (chapbook, with Denise Duhamel) (2000)

Exquisite Politics (with Denise Duhamel) (1997)

Co-edited

Reading Queer: Poetry in a Time of Chaos (with Neil de la Flor) (2018)

Saints of Hysteria: A Half-Century of Collaborative American Poetry (with Denise Duhamel & David Trinidad) (2007)

UNDERSEA

UNDERSEA

Maureen Seaton

For more information on this book or to order, visit www.jacklegpress.org.

Published by JackLeg Press
© 2021 Maureen Seaton
All rights reserved.
Printed in the United States of America.

ISBN: 978-1-7373307-0-7

No part of this work may be reproduced or publicized in any form or by any means, electronic or mechanical, including photocopying, microfilm, recording, or by any information storage and retrieval system, without permission in writing from the publisher. However, authors maintain ownership rights of their individual poems, and as such retain all rights to publish and republish their work.

Library of Congress Cataloging-in-Publication Data

Cover photo: Gauna, Ana Mercedes. Português: Naufrágio e recifes de coral no Nilo. March 2006. Wikimedia Commons.

Cover design by Jennifer Harris and Matthew Morse.

Reading Maureen Seaton's poems has always been a kind of astral projection for me. Reading *Undersea*, I was flung loose from my body so many times, sailing across the Sunshine State on a cloud of sensuous imagery. In Seaton's rendering of this land we love, "Avocados/fall like big and little bombs," "egrets grow fat on curly fries," and "there is no line between water and sky." Come for the "gibbous moonlight," the "canny pelicans," a "speedboat full of gangsters." Stay for the long-won wisdom of the poet herself, who hearkens Blake's imperative to "see the world in a grain of sand"--literally and figuratively, too. Seaton is the glass and the salt, the sling and the shot, "the blue ineffable" that lingers beyond her most luminous feats of language.

—Julie Marie Wade, author of *Same-Sexy Marriage: A Novella in Poems* and *Skirted*

For Lori Anderson

A man who is not afraid of the sea will soon be drowned, for he will be going out on a day he shouldn't. But we do be afraid of the sea, and we only be drowned now and again.

—John Synge, *The Aran Islands,* 1907

Contents

Rules for Cave Diving	1
A Dozen Poems…	4
Self-portrait with Avocado	5
Float	6
Of Lost Time	7
Sautéed Barnacles	8
Bigly in the Wild Weed	9
New Yorkers in Miami	10
A Pod of Whales	11
Jesus on the Beach	12
Tourist Season	13
Celestial Bodies	14
A Guide to Palmistry	15
Lemon Bay	16
Syncope	18
Salt	21
Vice	57
Self-portrait with Avocado and Yeats	58
Ghost Pepper	59
Autumn Triptych	60
Plumage and Flood	63

Florida	64
Snapper Creek Sonnet	65
Blowout	66
The Method of Vanishing Cues	67
Undertow	68
This Is Not America	69
I Swear There Were Oceans	70
A Thin Shining Place	71
The Mystery of the Direction of Time	72
Among Us, Divine	80
Biography	83
Acknowledgments	84

Rules for Cave Diving

Proceed until you find the end of the cave
or run out of air, whichever comes first.

Carve your initials in a rock with your dive knife
(holding your breath, if necessary).

Ignore the probability that truth is too mutable
to save you, spelunker.

(The hook, the spin, the last minute wishes.)

There's a shadow like a lobster without its shell,
ways you were terrified before, yet here you are.

Now follow the spin of your own dust out.
Remember you dropped stones to gauge depth?

They formed an altar at the mouth of the cave.
But that was long ago. Before you had lungs.

A Dozen Poems (I Mean Pelicans) Flew over My House Shouting Seaton (I Mean Sea) Stories

Since I'd never seen pelicans in flight, and only in photos, pouches
ballooning with bluefish, I was unprepared the first time I saw a dozen

glide in formation along the coast like pterodactyls or superheroes.
It was my first trip to Florida, and shorebirds were nothing but seagulls

to me then, foraging along the Hudson where I sat evenings until rats
came out chirping. All this hoopla about the "I" in poems boring readers

(the smart ones) (I'm told) to death. Someone's irked that I write about
my world and get away with it. (I'm not sure what I mean.) (Yes I am.) I've

lived in an efficiency for years with a mate whose night terrors are so loud
the dog and I huddle like orphans. My neighborhood borders the Atlantic,

it's true, and many have come here to die in brine, oldsters cocktailing
together, trembling the next day, sheepish and sunburned as folks stuck

in the same lifeboat. Still, I like my neighbors with their end-of-the-line
mentality—they feel real to me, sucking sea air and rum—and I drive

to work on a highway that keeps me on my toes, and I get to see brown
pelicans and kick up coral and sea beans along the surf. If I'm lonely,

with my salty neighbors and my traumatized mate who sings through the day
as if she hadn't been murdered in her sleep, it's the kind of lonely the sea

takes the edge off. Like going barefoot in wet sand until your feet glow.
Or walking to the end of the jetty and standing with the canny pelicans,

loving the warm sea back.

Self-portrait with Avocado

A vortex opens inside you,
sucks Florida right into you.

Sharks surround you
in your implausible bikini.

You sit beside a woman
whose plate holds the offal

of ripe fruit. Avocados
fall like big and little bombs.

Your head spins, green
with guacamole.

Float

This big sinking toe and its buoyant inhabitants.

When I first arrived I was shocked by two things: dinosaurs disguised as pelicans and men o' war disguised as dead balloons.

Either way I was naïve. I thought an ocean is an ocean and since I'd married the North Atlantic at seven, what could this lukewarm *lake* possibly have to offer me?

Years lapped by mathematically. I was a fractal and the seasons my humid iterations. I was predictable, the waves my loyal algorithms.

Last week I floated in the sea while a dozen gulls fought for a crust of pizza above me. When I looked up, the crust came plummeting down along with twelve unholy birds, like they were apostles and I was their lord.

Also: pirates and mermaids, pirates and mermaids, pirates and mermaids: they're real here.

Here is my creed: Fling yourself into the ocean, for it is loaded with salt. Float happy among the phosphorescent Floridians, their slick skin, their anemone hair.

May their tentacles surround you forever.

Of Lost Time
Miami Beach

Two French sisters die
beneath a dune buggy.

One is sleeping, the other
is reading Proust.

Sautéed Barnacles

The secret is simplicity. Flesh
of the delicate beast should be eaten
the day it's harvested. Just before
cooking, cut the beak free from the shell,
remove the throat, the roe, whatever else
lurks inside—need, diligence—and melt
butter in a small pan over medium
heat. Add wine, garlic, shallots. Do not brown.

Barnacles are hermaphroditic
so each has an ovary, which tastes
yummy—like the caviar of lobster fame.
Peel ovaries, retractor muscles, tear off
stubborn leathery stalks, chop parsley.
Ignore the hairy feet. Sauté. Serves two.

Bigly in the Wild Weed

> *Whose half-black hands assemble oranges*
> *is tom-tom hearted*
> *(goes in bearing oranges and boom).*
> —Gwendolyn Brooks, "The Second Sermon
> on the Warpland"

We're so in love lover you're the one whose
holy self tilts a rose-wise wish-hot half-black

planet on its punk-chin alarm side with hands
I could build an entire house with or assemble

a peace to write songs for or let's suck oranges
now before Florida floods and we're at sea. Is

it true we do exist without our former tom-tom
selves our ponderous hearts our swell hearted

old ghosts? I can't unimagine our croon it goes
zinging through love-beguiled blood our love in

the time of astonishment. What are we bearing
toward if not nothing recognizable our oranges

sap-bloody and sweet as all our only fruits and
everything bubble-upping bright sugar boom?

New Yorkers in Miami

First I'll make a stack of banana pancakes with bananas from our own
banana tree, then I'll ask you if a dip in the sea sounds good, because we live

near the sea now, and when we get home we'll make sandy love and lie like
raisins with kelpy hair in our hammock between gumbo limbo trees—come

on, let's go to the ocean, look! it's right there, I can see it out the fucking
window. And you look at me like you've been born a wise-ass, my own

special live-in wise-ass, all set to wise-ass me. People who live in Brooklyn
don't go to Coney Island, you say, and people who live in…wherever the

Grand Canyon is…don't go to the Grand Canyon either. And when you
think about it, you add, getting caught up in your own riff as if you're Walt

Whitman or someone alive good at making lists, all those people who live
near mountains don't ski! What mountains, I ask, in mild debunk mode,

though I agree in theory with your theory. Then our clothes come flying off
and our flip-flops flip, and we're running rowdy and buck wild into the

winter sea, goose-bumped and screaming, indisputable almost Floridians.

A Pod of Whales

A person can die of night terrors—right there in the middle of sleep, their hearts might stop, you say, as if I don't believe you. Sometimes you dream so loud your life flashes before my eyes, your screams raise ghost stories. Against my will, I am your wide-eyed witness. It's been years since we slept spooned and cozy, and I've almost forgotten I miss you. Still, I would go back to your race-betrayed American past and keep you safe from all the things a child should never have to see. You'd snore like any tired soul wrapped warm beside me, wake up yawning. Now a pod of pilot whales is stranded in shallows off the coast of Florida. They'll die together, it's true, as the pod will never abandon its wounded. Who can reconcile this cuspy hold on life, who sleep through the crescendo of hearts stopping?

Jesus on the Beach

Because I live on the beach in what some folks call old Florida, there have been a fair number of ponytailed guys in the neighborhood who resemble Jesus. One, in particular, drove a pick-up and loved animals, even beach cats. I don't know if my neighbor, Pete, was a poet or not. He looked like a middle-aged, hard-drugging Jesus to me, so he could have been. We said hi to each other most evenings, and if a hurricane came along, I knew he'd share his canned chili and Easy Cheese with me. One weekend he parked his truck crooked to keep tourists out of our little lot and he blocked my space by accident. When I politely tapped on his door to ask him to move his truck, he yelled from the shower: *Park on the goddamn grass, asshole.* His wife found him dead recently on the bathroom floor. He was shaving, she said, and he just keeled over. *Jesus*, I said to myself.

Tourist Season

Even surrounded by all these tourists you see the same beach folks all the time, like recognizable patches in a sandy quilt. You see them industrious and sweat-shined. You see them dripping with salt water. Mostly you see them leaning against lampposts on the Broadwalk (*sic*) and smoking on the sea wall, calling out your name as you approach in your magic cloak, which cloys horribly in the humidity and rarely gets you from here to there invisible, as promised.

Celestial Bodies

The second time someone stole my identity, my bank caught them right away. They liked to shop in Estero, Florida, a small town founded by Cyrus Teed in 1894, who theorized that celestial bodies are contained inside our hollow Earth. He also claimed to be immortal, which made his death in 1908 a great disappointment to his followers.

A Guide to Palmistry

My palm says life is short, health great. Or life goes on,
health's a crap shoot. The world spins lifelines around me—

they spiral off in all directions, bickering. Meanwhile, foot-long
lizards disguised as pirates contemplate a swim in a nearby

pool, lifelines flickering. Shorebirds poke around my feet,
their lines tiny, their minds poems. My intrepid Chihuahua

couldn't care less about his own lifeline, he assures me, only
mine. He drinks delicately from my cupped palm. Soon

we'll head home and the lizards will float comatose in chlorine,
egrets grow fat on curly fries. There must be some grace

for those with unreliable lifelines. Not a Sunday grace.
More the kind you get when you're flying across a highwire

thin as the line in your mutable disputable inscrutable palm.

Lemon Bay

Gulf

There is no line between water and sky. The seamless lay of all things blue. Yesterday a young man told his children that the best way to catch carp is to stick a small piece of seaweed on a hook and lower it into the carp's bed. Since carp prefer a clean bed, he said, they'll pick the seaweed up and get hooked. *Gotcha*, he said.

Midden

Everyone drives over the Calusa midden, underground store of shell and bone from dune to bay filled with discarded things, abandoned things, broken things. The storm flooded the midden last night. Now the earth slopes down to the bones and the memory of sun, the way it shone on people who once walked here with flesh and minds and tongues.

Gulf

This morning I open shutters and stare up at the Gulf of Mexico, risen above sea level in the stormy night. The waves are frantic, untimed, and local boys arrive to ride them. They know they'll get battered but they're jubilant with their boards under their arms. They were here until nightfall and here they are again.

Midden

I place a small whelk from the east coast on the midden to create a butterfly effect. Or to give something I love in return. Water everywhere. I can see and hear it on the Gulf side and I can see it glistening through the mangroves on the bay side. Lemon Bay. When the last native died, who buried her?

Gulf

Surfers swim out but are taken northwest too fast to stand up on their boards. People shell like mad. The day dawns bluer than yesterday.

Syncope

I have seen a scorpion so small it could fit beneath my tongue. The grace of a car in a cloverleaf, a floating city. Someone alive beneath the flood zone in what may remain of democracy. Even here, where pelicans burst in the air like blimps, one or more letters are lost in the interior of a word. The shadow of my head lies between the shadow of two palms. Little wind. Sweet weather. What kind of sail is that? Jib? Now my language faints in three syncopes: imagination, hierarchies, and all plans to the contrary. I ride down Dixie Highway and my DNA pops. Take that, I say, and something purls inside me and cleaves me with myth.

Salt

And Lot's wife, of course, was told not to look back where all those people and their homes had been. But she did look back, and I love her for that, because it was so human. So she was turned into a pillar of salt. So it goes.
—Kurt Vonnegut, Slaughterhouse-Five, 1969

I live ninety feet from the sea, amidst serious heat, near milky palms. Lot's wife walks stiffly past my window and the palms throw her an uninterested glance. If someone were to die out there, I would not hear her yell for help. (Hum of fan, drone of air conditioner.) She would see my light and look with hope toward my door, but her life would end soundlessly in the whir of everything I need to keep me cool.

☐

I've been instructed to observe my surroundings (not imagine them) and I've already messed up. So: There's a bowl of pears, a red lamp, and a tiny television that looks at me with its closed eye. A glass of tea teeters at the edge of a table my lover made in '88 on St. Mark's Place, where rats hovered in the ceiling above us, chirping.

□

My south window opens onto an old Florida beach street with colors of palm tree (like the one posing ironically in front of the house), mango (the motel across the street), and sky (which is everywhere as usual). From the window we move along the wall to the air conditioner, a fancy new one with little wings. Under the flap that moves up and down is a whole village of mold. The wall below the unit has gobs of Spackle put there over the months that the AC has been leaking, fixed, leaking. It's leaking right now, which explains the bowl of water beside the pears that ripen as the mold grows happily, and as the palm tree taunts and waves, speaking a language of its own, redolent of coconuts and fractured skulls.

◻

As far as I know, this efficiency where I live in four hundred square feet is not haunted. If there were ghosts I'd be able to tell. They're usually pretty selfish, as if they're the only ones entitled to their feelings.

□

My sister Z. hasn't talked to me in seven years. She sealed me off with the rest of the siblings inside our dad's green casket and left us to our violent heritage. When she was a kid she could put her hand in a swarm of bees and come away laughing. The only thing I ever remember her being afraid of was the palm tree.

☐

(According to Z.): Palm trees are fast on their feet, like roaches. They're trickster relatives of the great live oak or reincarnated Confederate soldiers. They throw coconuts at passersby, then straighten back up. They drop fronds on the side of the road that resemble dead animals or small children. They have very short roots, are admittedly dazzling in hurricanes, and the one outside my window is ignoring me so hard right now I can almost see its maniacal face.

□

It would be fun to reach for some watercolors right now. My brain is soggy with words. What part of the brain is responsible for metaphor? Is there anything in the middle of my right and left brain? A grayer area, a hybrid brain space? I'm reaching for watercolors. Drawing down the blue.

□

My daughters helped me find this little motel years ago. They flew in from Chicago after I'd looked for months, and we drove up and down the streets named for states and the streets named for presidents (American), and we saw a little sign with my landlord, Don's, number on it, and called. After that my hair grew long again and my eyes took in the world in a certain way hitherto unknown to me. I just wrote hitherto. Lot's wife walked by, laughing.

□

All the clocks say 11:42. L. loves clocks and mirrors. Time and reflection. I sit here for a few minutes thinking of what else to write. The word mirror is a good word. That is all I can think to say.

□

Now my hands move in slow-mo over these keys that look like the heads of South Florida ghost ants giving up their lives for me so that I may accomplish what I set out to do, which is a long something over several hours. My hands no longer say what I want them to say, but rather what they themselves believe they should say. As if they are two gods mapping out my life and I am their chauffeur.

☐

When my siblings and I were young, we had pet spiders that lived beneath the picnic table in a backyard that butted up against a wood on Long Island. The spiders were Daddy Long Legs and we played with them by letting them walk up and down our arms. We never tried to touch them. We simply sat next to them, under the table, and they would come and walk on us. Their eyes were too tiny to look into.

◻

*If I can't sleep tonight
I'll hover under the moon.*

~ Joseph Oets ~

☐

A woman walked across the moon of my dream last night covered in musical instruments, which has little to do with the external landscape of this transposed drawing experiment, where I'm supposed to look outside myself and write about what I see. But it has everything to do with what sings inside. Right now my dog is pressed against me, like a twin.

□

I used to think I couldn't be happy anywhere but on the Upper West Side yet I have not been able to get back there in twenty years twenty years twenty years twenty years twenty years twenty years. Someone taps me on the shoulder. The right one. I stop writing and take a drink of tea.

☐

I would like to write the way I used to without thought or punctuation my belly unknotted my eyes loose and see what happens if I follow the contours of some other dimension that lurks around this one pulling me into its orbit or dark matter or I am dark matter surrounded by Florida blue and light.

☐

The woman in my bed is restless. Her legs scissor and poke. She has promised to give me two more hours to myself. I will hold her to it without a guilty conscience because her stomach is full of my pancakes with blueberries and coconut milk. When we are together in bed we are young, or we are no age, or not in these bodies, or not on this planet, but in this rarified unconditional time that squeaks around and through us, pinning us here, souls in the grand flux, the blue ineffable.

☐

The palms outside the window move gracefully, full of grace. Perhaps because it is Sunday, I am connected to the idea of grace if not the practice. I woke with the word Septuagint flashing in my mind like a directional signal. I was excited to look it up and mildly disappointed when it turned out to be simply the Greek version of the Old Testament. Still, Septuagint led me to Polycarp of Smyrna and who can resist a word like Polycarp? And from Smyrna, no less, a little surfing town on the East coast of Florida.

☐

I myself was brought to this planet in the womb of Jersey's wetland along with my little brother. My sisters were lifted out of our mother's womb on the South Shore of Long Island—all of us born into salt.

☐

Now everyone is napping but me. L. snores lightly, her red glasses pushed up against her forehead, and the dog is curled against me like a comma. Although it is never quiet inside in the wet season, the conditioned air is the soundtrack for a restless peace. This room is green and white, the sheet below me a sea of fractals. If I believed in wishes, in this moment I would have none for myself. For others I would wish abundant food, abundant beauty, and for us all: the universal healing of bullies.

☐

Nevertheless, hours of writing, no matter how deeply it may touch the spirit of the writer, will not change the world more than a thin hair's worth. If this is not enough, I will write for another hour, and another, until the last monkey has washed his breakfast and looks up to see beside him, bending to the stream like a magnificent chorus, too many monkeys to count. I wonder if he will wonder how this miracle came to be, or if he'll simply shake his monkey head and take the first clean delicious bite.

☐

Light moves along the street from the ocean.

□

My sister got shot sometime in her thirties, though not fatally.

□

The moon loops around and heads backwards.
(Of course.)

□

One funny thing is that a lot of people think God is just for them personally. So, if both we and our enemies pray to Him, we believe He will listen to us and smite them, while, of course, they are thinking the same thing about us. (I just wrote smite.)

☐

Everyone wants me to move up the peninsula, across the country, or at least back to the Great Lakes or the Hudson Valley. For now, I tool along visiting them in my Honda. I weave in and out like blood around the body. I love to move this way, holding the wheel lightly.

□

My feet get cold when I write in air conditioning. I am suddenly self-conscious, as if someone might read this someday so maybe I should write something good enough for someone to read and enjoy. The first poet I ever met, named Ruth, became my teacher. She's the one who taught me to write without thinking someone might read it. I had a lot to say. I guess she knew I'd never say it if I thought for one minute someone would be listening. <Command Save>

☐

The woman in my bed plays a game on her computer even after her eyes are closed and her mouth has slackened in sleep. Her middle finger twitches up and down on her mouse. What game are you playing, honey, I ask her, and she answers, Sleep.

□

*Imagine words with a dimension
not unlike the light and dark regions
of the moon. The back of planets. The craters.
Words that orbit the body
like a plea granted.*

~ Kimiko Hahn ~

□

My parameters have been simple: write fifty poems in the same spot with the same view, for four hours. Otherwise, everything is allowed. For the first two hours, I sat alone. For the second two, I've had a small dog beside me, a warm brick. Sometimes I bend down and kiss his head where several strands of white sprout between his ears. He sleeps on, as if unqualifiedly safe.

□

Dear Z., I'm still in Florida where the palm trees frightened you and you vowed you'd never look at one again. Folks here are holdouts from when everything was lawless and there were cartels and motels and gin mills with ponytailed men throwing back shots and short beers. You were a great sister to tell a secret to. Here's one: A psychic told me you're still alive and somewhere cold. Here's another: I lied when I said the psychic said that. I've never talked to a psychic, but that's a lie too, as you know, and now the truth flies across the water like a speedboat full of gangsters. There are a dozen palm trees gathering at my window as I write this. They may be re-born Confederates, as you claim, or they may be genuine palm trees disguising the fact that you hide among them, the spine of your life pressed hard against mine.

☐

I picture the way various universes fold in on themselves to create more universes. How we're all folded up in here, waiting to reappear.

☐

I'm not sure what any of this says about me or the world, but it has never been noted anywhere before, and this seems like the right time: liminally speaking, between the ocean and the intracoastal, pinned to this island like a palm tree.

☐

I have no idea what I will do next.

☐

50 DRAWINGS IN 4 HOURS (Due Next Class)   100 points

Materials
-50 8.5x11" sheets of printer paper, NUMBERED on bottom right corner

-Any drawing media

Challenge! 50 drawings in 4 hours (time yourself if possible!): The purpose of this exercise is to sharpen your skills of observation and get really comfortable just drawing a lot (the average time you should spend on each drawing is about 5 minutes. If you spend 10 minutes on a drawing then you should do a bunch of quick 1 or 2 minute drawings). You can draw anything you want, in any observational (Blind Contour, Continuous Contour, Gesture, Full Value, etc.). I suggest you try all the styles, especially ones that seem more difficult. You should give yourself many different subjects to draw, and you can repeat anything you want. Look at everything around you, including objects, landscapes, people, etc. All 50 drawings MUST BE FROM LIFE - no Photographs or Ideas drawn from your imagination. You can draw in any media you want, even color, ball point pen, all drawing media, brush w/ ink or watercolor. The idea is that you are really developing your awareness of your surroundings and in your process through drawing and looking.

I know this may sound somewhat scary, but see it as an interesting challenge - remember you don't have to spend a lot of time on any one drawing, and they don't have to be great drawings, it is just about seeing- pure exercise and practice. There are usually a few really interesting drawings and some not so exciting. It's not about the quality as much as it is about the process of exploration.

All 50 are due next week, fewer than 50 will result in 0 points. They MUST be numbered 1-50.

Lea Anderson's Art Assignment

Vice

> *Women always think they're bulletproof.*—Secret Serviceman, Frank Wilson, regarding his wife, who was concerned that he was spending too much time away from home and suggested she accompany him on his surveillance of Al Capone. 1947

She walked down the beach at a good clip.
Black sneakers, anklets, a man's straw hat. He

was barefoot in Bermuda shorts and a fedora.
Small planes rhymed above the ocean. Terns

with crewcuts policed the shore. She wavered
in water and avoided a fine-trilled bone. He

fluctuated in the undertow like a circling rope.
A smear of sharks fifty feet from a smear of

bathers: what buzzes in the sargassum and
clinks in the heat—hustle, mob, midheaven,

underworld, bocci, Eliot Ness. Among the
dead, two were Leo, two Pisces, three Cancer,

and a Libra on the cusp. They all died tanning.

Self-portrait with Avocado and Yeats

Yeats preferred vampires
to ghosts, someone says.

The woman beside you
shrugs at metaphors.

Sharks surround you
in your implacable bikini. Yeats

makes you hungry, you say.
Florida crashes into you.

Ghost Pepper

Today I gave Haunted Ghost Pepper Tortilla
Chips to my fellow poets—accidentally, I

swear—chips made from peppers you should
only touch with gloves. *WTF,* said the poets,

tongues blazing, lips blistering. The peppers
were so ghostly nothing could cool the poets,

nothing douse the devil in their throats. Some
ran, some sat stoic as ghosts themselves until

there was a roaring like a poem no one had
ever heard. Gorgeous loud. *Portrait of the Artist*

loud. *Guinness Book of World Records* loud. I said,
When it gets too hot to swallow—spit it out.

Autumn Triptych

I. The Great Okeechobee Flood

1928, and I was not born yet. But I was here. A sigh in the leprous armadillo. A muñequito in a singer's lap. I know this song, I thought, and now I'm the music in wind and canal. I'm the elegant armadillo zooming whole along the floodplain. I wasn't born yet but I was here and I was here every year before and since. More than a spark, but like a spark, full of fire.

II. Parrots

It's the month of October when parrots sleep in the banyan trees. What this means is that if I lived elsewhere I'd be thinking about fall right now, not hurricanes. I'd be thinking about the reds, the mauves, the bittersweet, not getting ready for death, not listening to murmuring parrots in the never-falling canopy. They say falling leaves nourish the earth with their multi-colored deaths. This is comforting, if you stop to think about it.

III. Naranja

The opposite of naranja is not verde, as some would have us believe. Neither is naranja the cause or cure for melancolía de la tormenta, as others have written in quiet books about storm patterns that shatter color completely. No. (English.) No. (Español.) Naranja dissolves the distressed heart of melancolía in the same way it sweetens the blood—each drop peeled and dripping like a sugar skull in the sun.

Plumage and Flood

the city relights itself until it's time
for music to shiver the floorboards,
the hour of plumage...
—Lynda Hull

Somedays, I would rather be a light in the eye of any drab city than here in this dripping terrarium. Glistening web. Rampant glut. Today: an ostentation of peacocks on the causeway. Sandals sunk in sucking mud. Lives glossed in the wet. I think about the girl who died of beauty in this rain, her skin that shone with salt. Look outside the rattling doors, how the grass weeps in the flood. Shorebirds gurgle and mangroves swim away. I know someone is out there looking for her, boating slowly through glade, over hammock, reaching down to where the earth becomes the sea.

Florida

The dead rattle around in their underwater gear, praying,
debating—it's true, they link up in conga lines, assist

each other at births, smile toothless under black light. I love
them. I cannot love them enough. If I were to bring each one

surfside and pump them all back to life, they would surround
me like a swell of sailors, singing *way-aye, blow the man down.*

One autumn we were on 14th Street back North and you'd
forgotten your jacket. You said, *I have two dollars to my name*

and I'm going to buy myself a jacket, and you went into a store and
came out with a nice one. How did you do things like that?

There's a skeleton in the riptide. The storm's back wall blew
the letters off the Diane Motel. I'd been hiding in the eye and

thought: Damn, what will happen to the D? Now I'm heading
away from Tampa and Kissimmee. An old man hails a circus

train beside a cart of oranges. Oranges rule this state. They
control legislation and roll around like pointless politicians.

I once saw human sperm defrosting under a microscope,
just a drop of tadpoles, bumping hilariously into one another.

Snapper Creek Sonnet

Now I'm almost killed (again) on the Snapper
Creek Expressway, my shadow left behind on

blacktop like a map of this precarious sinking
city. So I invent an odd task for myself—

ephemera, I decide, harmless but illegal, that
tissue in felon wind, a blip beneath radar—

and I enjamb the law in small ways, felonious
poems sailing from the sealed lips of mermaid

sculptures, the tentacles of banyans, stuffed
into bottles I toss into Snapper Creek (the

creek, not the suicidal highway), begging fish,
fowl, and humankind: *O, Miami, save us.*

Blowout

She leaned over and lost her lunch in auburn
braids. She missed mermaid babies, their tiny

legs scalpeled into Levis. And mangroves, the
way they stood up for each other. Only a few

of the world's fittest fishes were left, scary
fishes, can't-eat-'ems. Women raced around

for a splash of passionflower water. They
were cosmetological. They rubbed together

like crickets. They behaved sanctimoniously.
She brought out the Caribbean gift set (value,

$100, reduced to $70). She fell asleep, selling.
Her throat opened like a gift certificate.

The Method of Vanishing Cues

I got myself a cup. It was the end of water
and I was the last to drink. I was

a revolver at the bed of the dead woman.
It was the cruel month and I was

inhabited by nightmares. It was a dream
the color of children. I was

taking off from MIA. It was the time we
drove in circles until we got there. I was

extinct in everglades. It was seasonable.
I skied through flambé or sorbet. I was

redhanded and tenderheaded. It was the best
and final cue. I broke into orchids and was gone.

Undertow
    after, and with a line by, Álvaro de Campos

It's said she leaves slick skin on the shore—
courted by mortals, she utters sons.

In this way, the Irish in her blood
boils up like soup (there are colors

of shrimp and atoll). Still, she longs
for the bloat of the deep, hair a tangle

of kelp, the dark entering her lungs,
algaed caves and phosphor.

Spread me over the sea, she prays,
where I can drown myself, if I like,

singing of all the things I will never live.

This Is Not America
(Bowie, 1985)

I must have played it a thousand times that summer, Gulf of Mexico, 2005—
to and from the mainland, up and down the coast in search of fossils.

I met a woman from Sarasota, a mad sea turtler who was allergic, as I was,
to the infamous red tide that arrived killing shellfish my third week on the key.

We couldn't breathe out there so we hunkered down where winged palmettos
perched along the rim of the kitchen at night and a ghost that resembled

Ralph Nader swam up and down the stairs while I tried to write—and I didn't
write much—red tide, turtles birthing, worst hurricane season in Atlantic history

starting up. They say that after Katrina a lot of Americans switched parties,
but it only lasted through one election. Sometimes sadness provides an entrance

to imagination. Other times it calls on a person to grieve. I was grieving in advance
that June. My heart was breaking as the first storm pounded the house with the dive-

bombing roaches and the impotent ghost—my American words holding their breath.

I Swear There Were Oceans

They say it takes three generations to build a house on the beach. Then it takes three more for the beach to dip coyly until the house is rendered uninhabitable.

Or habitable, if you are a sea creature.

Are you?

I imagine a woman lying on the sandbar tonight, right in front of me, as I walk fast, almost dancing, in earbuds. How her breath moves in one great puff toward the sea and grazes my feet in passing. *I'm gone*, she says, looking straight at me with her watery eye—*it's your turn*.

I swear there were oceans where there are now deserts, anemones spinning blood-red out to sea.

A Thin Shining Place

Mourning doves gorge on millet and sunflower seeds,
wings frantic around the feeder as if I've been starving them
for days, when, in fact, I've only been starving them for a day.

Sparrows hang back, afraid of trampling, and the glossy parrots
will be here as soon as the word is out, to pick the doves up
by the scruff of their necks and throw them into the ficus. For now,

the doves perch on the sill outside the window and look my cat
straight in the eye. He makes his angsty sound, a primal buzz
that the doves don't hear and, therefore, can't appreciate.

They flitter away at last, and I'm reminded of a meeting
twenty miles down the Florida pike, in which a brand new
poet from El Paso confessed that up until that rarefied time

the desire in his heart to write had been implacable.
It was my birthday, and I liked his gift, a card that glittered
with a mermaid holding anemones, not a wild parrot stealing

seed from the locals, not a thwarted cat or a diffident dove,
not a poem about birds and beach cats, not a poem at all, although
he would write them ruthlessly for the next two years then

go back home and take up the job of living a good one. He said,
I knew you liked shiny things, and of course I did. Now the parrots,
a dozen at least, arrive—hungry, selfish, neon thieves and princes.

The Mystery of the Direction of Time
Gulf of Mexico

She will be a sudden slanted lighthouse.

She will snorkel in the gulf, a wizened mermaid.

She will tend small fires, hiding them in pits along the beach.

She will sing in a way both pthalo blue and new-moonish.

She will stretch in a great heron pose, a long drink of seawater.

She will subsist on pine needles that grow on the dunes of the Gulf of Mexico some call the Lake.

She will draw a star map and leave her body for a certain time.

She will prepare a sarcophagus under the porch and slip inside where the iguana owns the right of way.

She will hear firecrackers deep in the mangroves. They will burn the roof of her mouth.

She will look at the water some call the Lake of Mexico and absorb its poisons and serenity.

She will read that Pisces rules the feet and paint her toenails blue.

She will adorn her neck with egg cases and tiny whelks.

She will blister from walking too far. Her hair will burn, a great flame so you can see her coming in the distance.

She will look at the horizon without longing.

~

She will look at the horizon and age suddenly. Her eyes will burst with
    longing.

She will plant her desires in the sand until she is finished with solitude.

She will walk five miles north, then south, before she opens her lunch and
    throws it to the gulls.

She will look out at the Gulf where the heron also looks and say I love you.
    The heron will not move, but the love will enter her like karma.

She will make sea grape jelly in a Popeye the Sailor pail.

She will invoke Lemon Bay and Manasota Key—places whose names are like
    lovers on her tongue.

She will claim Florida as her home though her past is the seed of a Northern
    island—long and full of crowds who drop their r's.

She will claim the Gulf as her mother, though she grew several leagues deep
    in the freezing North Atlantic.

She will stand among the mangroves and name their colors. Of the red, she
    will say their feet take them deep instead of far; of the black, she will say
    they wisely create forests of offsprings; of the white, she will say
    they bend over Lemon Bay like mothers.

~

She will hunch among the mangroves, a night heron.

She will write illegibly in tarpon and snook.

She will speak lemon shark and sand flea.

She will misunderstand the simplest of questions. For her name she will say Oystercatcher. For her address she will say here.

She will bicycle north on the mainland and on to Venice where they grow their own fossils: camel vertebrae and the enormous teeth of the carcharodon megalodon, the sixty-foot great white shark.

She will toss salads of gardenias and orange blossoms that taste of hurricanes.

She will run with naked legs to the rainbarrels and count her mosquito bites. They will number one hundred and fifty-seven.

She will sit on the mound of earth called the Calusa midden and sketch the ghosts as they float above the sand.

She will swim at Middle Beach at her own risk.

She will mourn the lizard who follows her into the hermitage and dies in the closet with the broom and the vacuum cleaner.

She will navigate insects. She will capture the largest and place them outside, where they will whisper and map their return.

~

She will find a ghost sleeping in her bed in cloud pajamas.

She will find a ghost on the screened-in porch, reading John Irving.

She will see a spirit moving along the road before he plunges into the mangroves.

She will lie down outside at night and look up. One star will shoot by, one will slay her.

She will wash her hair until it turns red with the blood of stars.

She will cut her hair and throw it onto the bones that have risen in the midden. She will watch it disappear and then she will recognize herself, but not always.

She will surround herself with mounds of poems, ghosts of stories. Writers will preach to her at night when there are no other sounds.

She will sleep the sleepless sleep of ghosts.

~

She will hunt for fossils on the north end of the key where the sand is black from the crushed bones of the Pleistocene.

She will bend to pick up teeth of a requiem shark, the barb of a stingray.

She will bless *Equus* and Mammoth, who once visited this place, like her.

She will feel the sea in the channels of her own bones where the nerves run up and down, making sense of all things.

She will fondle a sloth claw, fragments of a wolf tooth.

She will walk along the trough that lines the surf at low tide, searching for incisors.

She will hold the catfish spine in her hand and her hand will glow glacially. Ice sheets will slip down her sides and melt among her toes.

She will experience the Cenozoic as large cats move outside the hermitage, breathless from the mystery of the direction of time.

She will perch precariously on the line between dead and living, a line, she knows, that resembles the vein in her right wrist.

~

She will open her windows to sea sounds and when the sea comes close, she
   will remember the recent dead and the dead of thousands of years
   past.

She will grow to see in the dark.

She will wait for the loggerhead in gibbous moonlight.

She will notice that the moon is a three-quarter pearl.

She will notice that the moon is a seed with its mouth closed.

She will practice headstands, but only in her *mundus imaginalis*, her imaginary
   world. In her imaginary world she can last upside down for hours.
   Her head will open with light.

She will make a map of sea turtle tracks.

She will think about the ghost crabs running suicidally into the first storm of
   the season.

She will walk out to see them, into the storm called Arlene.

She will drag her body to the sea like a loggerhead and leave her babies
   behind to fend for themselves.

She will feel the twirl of her DNA inside her.

She will hear the music she makes as it ravels.

She will enter the Lake of the Gulf of Mexico headfirst and her flippers will
   work perfectly.

She will plan her return for the same time next year and will note it in her
   calendar in coconut milk and hibiscus.

~~

Among Us, Divine

I parted my own sea and you came to me: sort of unscripted, sort of splendid.
A loose bolt in the imagination—the very one that got me in trouble sipping

lilac wine (stolen from you five minutes ago). Remember? You were breaking
in your ukulele. All those tiny hand movements. I glued myself into a collage

and you flew. There was something old school about us. Or scientifically
unsound. We made faces at Czars. My eyes were browning then, and yours

were shaped like starfish. You never know who you'll run into as you sweep
the sea with a slender stalk. I've carried my life inside me for so long now,

never knowing where it would take me, so irretrievable, so stark raving mine.

Biography

Maureen Seaton pictured with Lori Anderson.

Maureen Seaton has authored twenty-two poetry collections, both solo and collaborative—most recently, *Sweet World* (CavanKerry, 2019), winner of the Florida Book Award in Poetry, and the chapbooks *Myth America* (Anhinga, 2020), co-written with Carolina Hospital, Nicole Hospital-Medina, and Holly Iglesias, and *Zero-Zero* (Hysterical Books, 2021), co-written with Kristine Snodgrass. Her honors include the NEA, Pushcart, and Lambda Literary Awards for *Furious Cooking* (Iowa, 1996) and *Sex Talks to Girls: A Memoir* (U. of Wisconsin, 2008, 2018). Her work has appeared in *Best American Poetry* and numerous anthologies and literary journals. Seaton is Professor of Creative Writing at the University of Miami and was voted Miami's Best Poet 2020 by *The Miami New Times*.

Acknowledgments

To the editors of the following publications, in which these poems first appeared, my deepest gratitude:

2 Bridges Review—"New Yorkers in Miami"

Court Green—"A Thin Shining Place"

Diode—"Ghost Pepper"

Green Mountains Review—"A Dozen Poems (I Mean Pelicans) Flew over My House Shouting Seaton (I Mean Sea) Stories," "Self-portrait with Avocado"

Jet Fuel Review—"Of Lost Time," as "Dune Buggy"

The Los Angeles Review Online—"Float"

Panhandler Magazine—"Snapper Creek Sonnet," "The Mystery of the Direction of Time," "Blowout," "Vice," "Self-portrait with Avocado and Yeats"

Pea River Journal—"Plumage and Flood"

Pleiades—"This Is Not America"

Saw Palm—"Salt," "Syncope" (excerpted from "Five Minutes to the End of Time")

South Florida Poetry Journal—"A Pod of Whales," "Jesus on the Beach"

Spelunker Flophouse—"Barnacles"

SWWIM Every Day—"Among Us, Divine"

TriQuarterly—"The Method of Vanishing Cues"

Wisconsin Review—"Undertow"

"Bigly in the Wild Weed" appeared in *The Golden Shovel Anthology*.

"Snapper Creek Sonnet" was reprinted in *Sinking City*.

"Blowout" also appeared in the chapbook, *Tit, with Blue Guitar*, from Dancing Girl Press.

"The Mystery of the Direction of Time" was reprinted in the catalogue for "Change Agents," an art show curated by Michelle Weinberg for Girls' Club, South Florida, 2017.

"Rules for Cave Diving," which was originally published in *Cave of the Yellow Volkswagen* (Maureen Seaton, Carnegie Mellon University Press, 2009), won the Broadsided Press "Switcheroo: 2016" and was printed on a broadside with Jennifer Bevill's image, "Undersea," for which this collection is gratefully named.

A small section of "Salt" was reprinted on a broadside by Tom Virgin, Extra Virgin Press, Miami, in his series, "Miami 100." Thanks, Tom!

Thanks to visual artist Lea Anderson for creating the assignment, "50 Drawings in 4 Hours," for her art students in Albuquerque, NM. And to Sarah Gamoke, for sharing it with me so I could alter it for poets and write "Salt."

And thanks to Bruce Rodgers, director of the Hermitage Artist Retreat on Manasota Key, Florida, for the glorious month of June 2005, where "The Mystery of the Direction of Time" was conceived and written.

OTHER TITLES FROM JACKLEG PRESS

jacklegpress.org

Under the Hours. Barbara Cully

Two Thieves and a Liar. Neil de la Flor, Maureen Seaton, and Kristine Snodgrass

Hallucinogenesis. D.C. Gonzales-Prieto

Trapline. Caroline Goodwin

This is How I dream It. Jennifer Harris

Men in Correspondence. Meagan Lehr

Observations of an Orchestrated Catastrophe. Jenny Magnus

when i am yes. cin salach

Genetics. Maureen Seaton

The War on Pants. Kristine Snodgrass

www.ingramcontent.com/pod-product-compliance
Lightning Source LLC
Chambersburg PA
CBHW020912080526
44589CB00011B/560